Richard Lederer's
Classic Literary Trivia

Richard Lederer's
Classic Literary Trivia

By Richard Lederer

Illustrations by Barry Blitt

Gibbs Smith, Publisher

TO ENRICH AND INSPIRE HUMANKIND

Salt Lake City | Charleston | Santa Fe | Santa Barbara

First Edition
11 10 09 08 07   5 4 3 2 1

Text © 2007 Richard Lederer
Illustrations © 2007 Barry Blitt

Published by
Gibbs Smith, Publisher
P.O. Box 667
Layton, Utah 84041

Orders: 1.800.835.4993
www.gibbs-smith.com

Designed by Kurt Wahlner
Printed and bound in United States of America

Library of Congress Cataloging-in-Publication Data

Lederer, Richard, 1938-
Richard Lederer's classic trivia / Richard Lederer ; illustrations by
Barry Blitt. — 1st ed.
    p. cm.
ISBN-13: 978-1-4236-0212-5
ISBN-10: 1-4236-0212-9
1. Literature—Miscellanea. 2. Civilization, Classical—Miscellanea. I.
Title.

PN43.L38 2007
800–dc22

20070π03008

To the Szeto family
and their good lives
with the Good Book

Contents

Introduction

Not long ago, officials from Mainland China offered a pair of pandas to the people of Taiwan. The Taiwanese populace swooned over the gift, but the island's president, Chen Shui-bian, urged his government to say no, fearing that the cute bundles of fur would turn out to be "Trojan pandas."

For years, a satirical virus warning has whizzed around the Internet:

Hey Hector,

This was forwarded to me by Cassandra—it looks legit. Please distribute to Priam, Hecuba, and your 99 siblings.

—Thanks, Laocoön

Warning! Warning! Warning!

If you receive a gift in the shape of a large wooden horse, do not download it! It is extremely destructive and will overwrite your entire city!!!

The 'gift' is disguised as a large wooden horse about two stories tall. It tends to show up outside the city gates and appears to be abandoned. Do not let it through the gates! It contains hardware that is incompatible with Trojan programming, including a crowd of heavily armed Greek warriors that will destroy your army, sack your town, and kill your women and children. If you have already received such a gift, do not open it! Take it back out of the city unopened and set fire to it by the beach.

Forward this message to everyone you know!

The fullest effect of President Shui-bian's comment about "Trojan pandas" and the Internet virus joke is achieved only if the reader knows something about the decade-long Trojan War, chronicled in the Greek poet Homer's epic, *The Iliad*.

Priam and Hecuba were king and queen of Troy and their son Hector its bravest defender. In an effort to win the war, the Greeks sent a huge wooden horse to the Trojans as an offering to Athena. Inside the horse were hiding a host of soldiers. The priest Laocoön tried to warn the Trojans to beware of Greeks bearing gifts but was killed by two giant serpents. Later, the Greek soldiers emerged from the horse by night and overthrew Troy.

Allusions allow us to experience an idea on two levels at once by linking what we are reading or hearing with what we have read or heard in the past. Such references enhance the present through experiences that glow through time. Our lives are considerably enriched when we are able to identify such references because allusions play an important role in creating impressions and emotions.

The more you learn about the references and allusions that knit us together as a civilization, the more deeply you will live—and the more you will understand and laugh. *Classic Literary Trivia* will test your knowledge of our civilization's three richest and most luminous sources of allusions—the Bible, Greek mythology, and the works of William Shakespeare.

The Roman poet Lucretius explained his method of teaching in his poem "The Nature of Things." He said that he treated the passing along of academic subject matter in the same way that a physician, intending to administer medicine, might coat the rim of the cup with honey. Play is the honey of this book. As you have fun with games and quizzes about classic literature, I hope that you will be inspired to read or reread some of the masterpieces mentioned along the way. If you are, run—don't walk—to your nearest library.

Richard Lederer
San Diego, California
richard.lederer@pobox.com

The
Bible

In Their Own Words

The word *bible* derives from the Greek *biblia*, which means "books." Indeed, the Bible is a whole library of books that contains many different kinds of literature—history, narrative, short stories, poetry, philosophy, riddles, fables, allegories, letters, and drama. Many parts of the Bible are highly dramatic because they show in detail the sweep of grand events as experienced by a vivid and diverse cast of persons.

As their hopes and fears, ambitions and tragedies, and laughter and sorrows unfold in the Bible, many of these men and women have become so familiar to so many readers that they have become archetypal. Thus, a large man is a Goliath, an old man a Methuselah, a wise man a Solomon, a traitorous man a Judas, an evil woman a Jezebel, a doer of good deeds a good Samaritan, a patient man a Job, a skeptical man a doubting Thomas, a mighty hunter a Nimrod, and a strong man a Samson (while his luggage is Samsonite).

Many of these people reveal themselves through what they say. From their own words, identify these biblical personages:

1. "Am I my brother's keeper?"

2. "For whither thou goest I will go; and where thou lodgest, I will lodge; thy people shall be my people, and thy God my God."

3. "Let my people go."

4. "O my son Absalom! my son, my son Absalom! would God I had died for thee, O Absalom, my son, my son!"

5. "My God, my God, why hast thou forsaken me?"

6. "O Lord God, remember me, I pray thee, and strengthen me, I pray thee, only this once,

O God, that I may be at once avenged of the Philistines for my two eyes."

7. "Naked came I out of my mother's womb, and naked shall I return thither: the Lord gave, and the Lord hath taken away; blessed be the name of the Lord."

8. "Take me up, and cast me forth into the sea; so shall the sea be calm unto you: for I know that for my sake this great tempest is upon you."

9. "My God hath sent his angel, and hath shut the lions' mouths, that they have not hurt me."

10. "Thou art the man. Thus saith the Lord God of Israel, I anointed thee king over Israel, and I delivered thee out of the hand of Saul."

11. "Divide the living child in two, and give half to the one, and half to the other."

12. "Why have ye conspired against me, thou and the son of Jesse?"

13. "After I am waxed old shall I have pleasure, my lord being old also?"

14. "Behold the fire and the wood: but where is the lamb for a burnt offering?"

15. "The serpent beguiled me, and I did eat."

16. "Feed me, I pray thee, with that same red pottage, for I am faint."

17. "Hereby ye shall know that the living God is among you, and that he will without fail drive out from before you the Canaanites."

18. "Am I not a Philistine, and ye servants to Saul? Choose you a man for you, and let him come down to me. If he be able to fight with me, and to kill me, then will we be your servants."

19. "Take ye him, and crucify him: for I find no fault in him."

20. "If it please the king, and if I have found favor in his sight, and the thing seem right before the king, and I be pleasing in his eyes, let it be written to reverse the letters devised by Haman the son of Hammedatha the Agagite, which he wrote to destroy the Jews which are in all the king's provinces."

21. "I am Esau, thy firstborn; I have done according as thou badest me: arise, I pray thee, sit and eat of my venison, that thy soul may bless me."

22. "Now therefore be not grieved, nor angry with yourselves, that ye sold me hither: for God did send me before you to preserve life."

23. "I do not know the man."

24. "The woman whom thou gavest to be with me, she gave me of the tree, and I did eat."

25. "Behold, I have hearkened unto your voice in all ye said unto me, and have made a king over you."

26. "One basket had very good figs, even like the figs that are first ripe: and the other basket had very naughty figs, which could not be eaten, they were so bad."

27. "I have sinned in that I have betrayed the innocent blood."

28. "Curse God, and die."

29. "What have I done to thee, that thou hast smitten me these three times?"

30. "Go and search diligently for the young child; and when ye have found him, bring me word again, that I may come and worship him also."

Answers

1. Cain. Genesis 4:9. 2. Ruth. Ruth 1:16. 3. Moses. Exodus 5:1. 4. David. II Samuel 18:33. 5. Jesus. Mark 15:34. 6. Samson. Judges 16:28. 7. Job. Job 1:21 8. Jonah. Jonah 1:12 9. Daniel. Daniel 6:22. 10. Nathan. II Samuel 12:7.

11. Solomon. 1 Kings 3:25. 12. Saul. I Samuel. 22:13. 13. Sarah. Genesis 18:12. 14. Isaac. Genesis 22:7. 15. Eve. Genesis 3:13. 16. Esau. Genesis 25:30. 17. Joshua. Joshua 3:10. 18. Goliath. I Samuel 17:8–9. 19. Pontius Pilate. John 19:6. 20. Esther. Esther 8:5.

21. Jacob. Genesis 27:19. 22. Joseph. Genesis 45:5. 23. Peter. Matthew 26:72. 24. Adam. Genesis 3:12. 25. Samuel. I Samuel 12:1. 26. Jeremiah. Jeremiah 24:2. 27. Judas. Matthew 27:4. 28. Job's wife. Job 2:9. 29. Balaam's ass. Numbers 22:28. 30. Herod. Matthew 2:8.

Bible by the Numbers

"In a hundred years the Bible will be a forgotten book found only in museums," predicted French author Voltaire, writing from his home in Geneva. A century later his home was owned and occupied by the Geneva Bible Society.

The thirty-nine books of the Old Testament, the twenty-seven books of the New Testament, and the fifteen books of the Apocrypha compose the champion bestseller of all time. Translated into more than 2,000 languages, the Bible is available to about 80 percent of the world's people and outsells all other popular books. Each year, in the United States alone, approximately 44 million copies are sold and 91 million distributed.

With those vital statistics in mind, try your hand and memory at playing a numbers game about the Bible:

1. How many books of the Bible are named after women?

2. How many days did it take God to create the world?

3. How many times are the words *apple, snake,* and *whale* mentioned in the Bible versions of Genesis and Jonah?

4. How many rivers were there in Eden?

5. How long did Methuselah live?

6. How many cubits in length did God command Noah to build the ark?

7. How many of each animal went onto the ark?

8. How long did the flood last?

9. God agreed to spare Sodom and Gomorrah if Abraham could find how many righteous people there?

10. How old was Abraham when his son Isaac was born?

11. How many patriarchs were there?

12. How many brothers did Joseph have?

13. How many cows were in the dream that Pharaoh related to Joseph?

14. How many tribes of Israel were there?

15. How many plagues were visited on the Egyptians because Pharaoh would not let the people of Israel go?

16. How many years did Israel wander in the desert?

17. How many commandments did God deliver to Moses on Mount Sinai?

18. How many times did Balaam smite his ass?

19. How many days did Joshua and his army circle Jericho, blowing their trumpets at its walls?

20. How many men did Samson slay with the jawbone of an ass?

21. How long did Solomon rule over Israel?

22. How many wives and how many concubines did Solomon have?

23. How long did Jonah remain in the belly of the fish?

24. How many comforters did Job have?

25. According to the Psalms, how many years are allotted to each human being?

26. Which psalm begins, "The Lord is my shepherd; I shall not want. He maketh me to lie down in green pastures"?

27. Of how many beasts did Daniel dream?

28. How many friends of Daniel were cast into the fiery furnace but saved by God?

29. How many gospels are there in the Bible?

30. How many months older than Jesus was John the Baptist?

31. How many brothers did Jesus have?

32. How many apostles did Jesus recruit?

33. How many days did Jesus fast in the desert?

34. How many parables of Jesus are there in the Bible?

35. How many men did Jesus feed with how many loaves and how many fishes?

36. How many men passed by the injured man before the Samaritan stopped to help?

37. In the parable of the workers in the vineyard, at what hour were the last workers hired?

38. For how many days had Lazarus been dead before being raised by Jesus?

39. In Jesus's parable of the virgins, how many virgins were there? How many were wise and how many foolish?

40. By the end of the parable of the talents, how many talents had the man who had originally been given five?

41. How many Beatitudes did Jesus deliver?

42. With how many thieves was Jesus crucified?

43. How many hours did Jesus hang on the cross before he died?

44. How many pieces of silver were given for Judas's betrayal?

45. How many times did Peter deny Jesus?

46. How many Marys told of Jesus's resurrection?

47. How many days occurred between his death and his resurrection?

48. The Book of Revelation mentions a scroll closed with how many seals?

49. How many Horsemen of the Apocalypse were there?

50. What is the Number of the Beast?

Answers

1. Two in the Old Testament—Ruth and Esther; two in the Apocrypha—Judith and Susanna. 2. Six. Genesis 1:31. 3. Zero. *Fruit, serpent,* and *great fish* are mentioned a number of times. 4. Four. Genesis 2:10. 5. 969 years. Genesis 5:27. 6. Three hundred. Genesis 6:15. 7. Two. Genesis 7:14–16. But note Genesis 7:2–3, which numbers the clean beasts and fowls of the air by sevens. 8. Forty days (Genesis 7:17) but note "And the waters prevailed upon the earth a hundred and fifty days" (Genesis 7:24). 9. Ten. Genesis 18:32. 10. One hundred years old. Genesis 21:5.

11. Three: Abraham, Isaac, and Jacob. 12. Eleven. Genesis 35:22. 13. Fourteen; seven fat and seven lean. Genesis 41:17–20. 14. Twelve. Genesis 49:28. 15. Ten. Exodus 7–11. 16. Forty. Joshua 5:6. 17. Ten. Exodus 20:3–17. 18. Three. Numbers 22:28. 19. Seven. Joshua 6:14–15. 20. A thousand. Judges 15:15.

21. Forty years. I Kings 11:42. 22. Seven hundred and three hundred. I Kings 11:3. 23. Three days and nights. Jonah 1:17. 24. Three. Job 2:11. 25. Seventy. Psalms 90:10. 26. The twenty-third. 27. Four. Daniel 7:3–7. 28. Three. Daniel 3:19. 29. Four. 30. Six. Luke 1:26.

31. Four: James, Joses, Judas, and Simon. Mark 6:3. 32. Twelve. Matthew 10:2. 33. Forty. Matthew 4:2. 34. Believe it or not, sixty-four. 35. Five thousand, with five loaves and two fishes. Mark 6:38 and 6:44, Luke 9:13–14, John 6:9–10. 36. Two. Luke 10:31–32. 37. The "eleventh hour." Matthew 20:6. 38. Four. John 11:17. 39. Ten: five wise and five foolish. Matthew 25:1–2. 40. Eleven. Matthew 25:28.

41. Nine. Matthew 5:3–11. 42. Two. Mark 15:27. 43. Six. Mark 15:25 and 15:34. 44. Thirty. Matthew 26:15, 27:3. 45. Three. Matthew 26:69–75. 46. Two: Mary Magdalene and Mary the mother of James. Luke 24:10. 47. Three. Matthew 27:63. 48. Seven. Revelation 5:1, 8:1. 49. Four. Revelation 6:2–8. 50. 666. Revelation 13:18.

Bible
Riddles

Riddles are perhaps the most ancient of all verbal puzzles, dating back at least 2,500 years. The most famous riddle of all is the one that the Sphinx put to Oedipus: "What goes on four legs in the morning, on two at noon, and on three at night?" Oedipus, one of the first game show contestants, answered the riddle correctly and thus became Oedipus Rex. His solution: "Man: in infancy, he crawls; in his prime, he walks; in old age, he leans on a staff."

In the biblical Book of Judges, the mighty Samson comes upon a swarm of bees making honey in the carcass of a lion. From this, Samson makes a bet with the Philistines that they cannot solve his original riddle: "Out of the eater came forth meat, and out of the strong came forth sweetness." After seven days of weeping, Samson's wife wheedles the answer out of him and conveys it to the Philistines. In a rage, Samson kills thirty of them and lays waste their city. Today we don't take riddles quite as seriously, but we do derive sweetness and strength from a cleverly turned poser.

The Bible has inspired not only an outpouring of great literature, art, and music but also an impressive array of riddles based on its stories. The canon of biblical riddles reminds us that we can laugh with the Bible as well as learn from it:

1. When was baseball first played in the Bible?

2. What animals disobeyed God's command to "be fruitful and multiply"?

3. Who was the champion runner of all time?

4. What was the longest day in the Bible?

5. At what time of day was Adam created?

6. Why couldn't Eve have measles?

7. Did Eve ever have a date with Adam?

8. On what did the earliest people do arithmetic lessons?

9. How were Adam and Eve prevented from gambling?

10. What did Adam and Eve never have but left to their children?

11. What evidence is there that Adam and Eve were pretty noisy?

12. How long did Cain hate his brother?

13. When was meat first mentioned in the Bible?

14. What animal took the most baggage into the ark; what animals took the least?

15. Why weren't there any worms in the ark?

16. What creatures were not on the ark?

17. Where did Noah keep the bees?

18. Who was the best financier in the Bible?

19. Where did all the people in the world hear one rooster crow?

20. Why couldn't people play cards on the ark?

21. Where was Noah when the lights went out?

22. Why couldn't Noah catch many fish?

23. When is paper money first mentioned in the Bible?

24. What did the cat say when the ark landed?

25. Why was Lot's wife turned into a pillar of salt?

26. When was tennis first played?

27. Who was the straightest man in the Bible?

28. How was Pharaoh's daughter like a stockbroker?

29. What did the Egyptians do when it got dark?

30. Who was the first man in the Bible to break all ten commandments?

31. How do we know for certain that Moses was a male?

32. Who were the three most constipated men in the Bible?

33. Who was the greatest actor in the Bible? What did he die of?

34. How was Ruth rude to Boaz?

35. Why was Goliath astonished when David hit him with a stone?

36. Who was older—David or Goliath?

37. What evidence is there of sewing in the time of David?

38. Why was the prophet Elijah like a horse?

39. Who was the most successful doctor in the Bible?

40. What did Job have to cover his sackcloth and ashes?

41. Who was the strongest man in the Bible?

42. Who was Jonah's guardian?

43. How is the story of Jonah an inspiration?

44. How was John the Baptist like a penny?

45. Who were the three tiniest apostles?

46. Who set the record for the high jump in the Bible?

47. How was St. Paul like a horse?

48. How was a baseball game played in the Bible?

49. Who were the shortest men in the Bible?

50. What three noblemen are mentioned in the Bible?

Answers

1. In the big inning. 2. adders 3. Adam. He was the first in the human race. 4. The one with no Eve. 5. A little before Eve.

6. Because she'd Adam. 7. No, it was an apple. 8. God told them to multiply on the face of the earth. 9. They lost their paradise. 10. Parents.

11. They raised Cain. 12. As long as he was Abel. 13. When Noah took Ham into the ark. 14. The elephant took his trunk, but the fox and the rooster took only a brush and comb between them. 15. Because worms come in apples, not in pairs.

16. Fish. 17. In the ark hives. 18. Noah. He floated his stock while the whole world was in liquidation. 19. In the ark. 20. Noah sat on the deck.

21. In d'ark. 22. He only had two worms. 23. When the dove brought the green back to the ark. 24. Is that Ararat? 25. Because she was dissatisfied with her Lot.

26. When Joseph served in Pharaoh's court. 27. Joseph. Pharaoh made a ruler out of him. 28. She took a little prophet from the rushes on the banks. 29. They turned on the Israelites. 30. Moses.

31. He wandered around the desert for forty years and never stopped to ask anyone for directions. 32. Cain, because he wasn't Abel; Methuselah, who sat on the throne for 900 years; and Moses, because God gave him two tablets and sent him into the wilderness. 33. Samson. He brought down the house, then died of fallen arches. 34. She pulled his ears and stepped on his corn. 35. It had never entered his head before.

36. David. He rocked Goliath to sleep. 37. He was hemmed in on all sides. 38. He was fed from aloft. 39. Job. He had the most patience. 40. Only three miserable comforters.

41. Jonah. The whale couldn't keep him down. 42. The whale brought him up. 43. Jonah was down in the mouth but came out all right. 44. He was one sent. 45. Peter, James, and John. They all slept on a watch.

46. Jesus, when he cleared the temple. 47. He liked Timothy, hey? 48. In the big inning, Eve stole first, Adam stole second, Rebecca walked with the pitcher, Gideon rattled the pitchers, Saul was put out by David, Absalom and Judas went out swinging, and the prodigal son stole home. 49. It is commonly believed that they were Knee-high Meyer and Bildad the Shuhite (shoe height), but Paul said, "Silver and gold have I none," and no one could be shorter than that. 50. Barren fig tree, Lord how long, and Count thy blessings.

Good Words From the Good Book

A front-page story in a St. Louis newspaper reported an incident in which two men were hospitalized after a fistfight. An automobile had stopped for a red light at a main intersection. A man on the sidewalk called out to its driver, "Hey, Mister, your left front tire is going flat." The driver got out, looked at the tire, and called to his benefactor, "Thanks for being a good Samaritan!" Whereupon the pedestrian leaped off the curb and started pounding the driver with his fists, shouting, "You can't call me a dirty name." The shocked driver struck back, and the result was that both men ended up in the hospital—all because one of them thought that being identified as a "Samaritan" was an insult.

Few of us will end up eating a knuckle sandwich because we miss the source of a biblical allusion—in this case, Luke 10:30–37. But our lives are considerably enriched when we are able to identify such sources, because allusions become keys that unlock the doors to many mansions—itself a biblical reference to John 14:2, where Jesus says, "In my Father's house are many mansions."

While the spiritual values of the Bible are almost universally recognized, the enduring effect of the Bible on the English language is often overlooked. The fact is, though, that a great number of biblical words, references, and expressions have become part of our everyday speech so that even people who don't read the Bible carry its text on their tongues.

Identify the biblically inspired words described below:

1. In ancient times, a _____ was a unit of weight, and this weight of silver or gold constituted a monetary unit, one that figures promi-

nently in a famous parable of Jesus: "For the kingdom of heaven is as a man travelling into a far country, who called his own servants, and delivered unto them his goods. And unto one he gave five _____, to another two, and to another one; to every man according to his several ability" (Matthew 25:14–15).

The most common modern meaning of the word _____—some special, often God-given ability or aptitude—is a figurative development from the parable.

2. An obstacle: "Thou shalt not curse the deaf, nor put a _____ before the blind, but shalt fear thy God" (Leviticus 19:14).

3. A special celebration: "And ye shall hallow the fiftieth year, and proclaim liberty throughout all the land unto all the inhabitants thereof: it shall be a _____ unto you" (Leviticus 25:10).

4. "Now when Jesus was risen early the first day of the week, he appeared first to Mary Magdalene, out of whom he had cast seven devils. And she went and told them that had been with him, as they mourned and wept" (Mark 16:9–10). Mary Magdalene became a favorite subject of medieval and Renaissance painters,

who traditionally depicted her as weeping. The tearful Mary was portrayed so sentimentally that, over the years, her name has been transformed into the word _____, which has come to mean "tearfully sentimental."

5. A final, decisive battle, marked by overwhelming slaughter: "And he gathered them together into a place called in the Hebrew tongue _____. . . . And there were voices, and thunders, and lightnings; and there was a great earthquake, such as was not since men were upon the earth, so mighty an earthquake, and so great" (Revelation 16:16,18).

6. Anything of enormous size: "Behold now _____, which I made with thee. . . . Behold, he drinketh up a river and hasteth not: he trusteth that he can draw up Jordan into his mouth" (Job 40:15, 23).

7. Anything of enormous size: "In that day the Lord with his sore and great and strong sword shall punish _____ the piercing serpent, even _____ that crooked serpent; and he shall slay the dragon that is in the sea" (Isaiah 27:1).

8. "How doth the city sit solitary, that was full of people! How is she become as a widow! She

that was great among the nations, and princess among the provinces, how is she become tributary!"

This is a typically dark passage in one of the prophetic books, from which we derive the word _____, meaning a sorrowful tirade, extended lament, or bitter denunciation.

9. "Then the Lord of the _____ gathered them together for to offer a great sacrifice unto Dagon their god, and to rejoice" (Judges 16:23).

Because the nation described above were an alien, non-Semitic people who worshiped strange gods, their name became a term for a foreigner. Nineteenth-century philosophers, such as Thomas Carlyle and Matthew Arnold, further changed the meaning of the word so that today _____ is a derogatory term for one who shuns intellectual and cultural activities.

10. In Judges 12:5–6, we learn about a conflict between the peoples of Gilead and Ephraim: "And the Gileadites took the passages of Jordan before the Ephraimites; and it was so, that when those Ephraimites which were escaped said, Let me go over; that the men of Gilead said unto him, Art thou an Ephraimite? If he said, Nay;

then they said unto him, Say now _____"
(Judges 12:5–6).

Because the Ephraimites didn't have the *sh* sound in their language, they could not pronounce the word correctly, and 42,000 of them were slain. That's how the word _____ has acquired the meaning that it has today: a password, catchword, or slogan that distinguishes one group from the other.

Answers

1. talent 2. stumbling block 3. jubilee 4. maudlin 5. armageddon 6. behemoth 7. leviathan 8. jeremiad 9. philistine 10. shibboleth

Holy Moses!

Along with the works of William Shakespeare, the Bible is the most fruitful source of everyday phrases in the English-speaking world. Exclamations like "Holy Moses!" and "Judas Priest!" are the most obvious, but there are tens of other biblical phrases that season our speech.

Many such expressions are direct borrowings, such as "kingdom come," in Matthew 6:10, and "the eleventh hour," from Matthew's version of Jesus's parable of the workers in the vineyard who gained employment so late in the day (Matthew 20:6).

Others have entered our modern idiom in a slightly revised form, as "crystal clear" (from "clear as crystal" in Revelation 22:1) and "by the skin of my teeth." The latter echoes Job's lament in Job 19:20. "My bone cleaveth to my skin and to my flesh, and I am escaped with the skin of my teeth" ("by the skin of my teeth" in the Revised Standard Version). "But teeth don't have any skin," you protest. In the biblical phrase, the "skin" refers to a margin of safety as thin as the enamel on the teeth.

In the Song of Solomon 7:4, the beloved is told, "Thy neck is as a tower of ivory." From this comparison derives the modern cliché "an ivory tower," which picks up the sense of beauty, loftiness, and unassailability implied by the original words.

Still other expressions are general references to a biblical story, like "to raise Cain" and "Adam's apple," so called because many men, but few women, exhibit a bulge of laryngeal cartilage in front of their throats. According to male-dominated folklore, Eve swallowed her apple without care or residue, while a chunk of the fruit stuck in the throat of the innocent and misled Adam.

Here, listed in the order they occur in the Bible, are fifty biblical turns of phrase that have survived the centuries pretty much unscathed. Complete each item:

1. Saw the _____ (Genesis 1:4)
2. My brother's _____ (Genesis 4:9)
3. Sold his _____ for a mess of _____ (Genesis 25:33–34)
4. The _____ of the land (Genesis 45:18)
5. A land flowing with _____ and _____ (Exodus 3:17)
6. Man doth not live by _____ alone (Deuteronomy 8:3)
7. The _____ of his eye (Deuteronomy 32:10)
8. A hair's _____ (Judges 20:16)
9. A man after his own _____ (I Samuel 13:14)
10. Played the ____ (I Samuel 26:21)
11. A still small _____ (I Kings 19:12)
12. Weeping and _____ (Esther 4:3)
13. Give up the _____ (Job 3:11)
14. In the land of the _____ (Job 28:13)

15. Out of the mouths of _____ (Psalms 8:2)

16. His heart's _____ (Psalms 10:3)

17. At their wit's _____ (Psalms 107:27)

18. Labor in _____ (Psalms 127:1)

19. Out of the _____ (Psalms 130:1)

20. Pride goeth. . . before a _____ (Proverbs 16:18)

21. Vanity of _____ (Ecclesiastes 1:2)

22. There is nothing new under the _____ (Ecclesiastes 1:9)

23. Eat, drink, and be _____ (Ecclesiastes 8:15)

24. As white as _____ (Isaiah: 1:18)

25. They shall beat their _____ into _____ (Isaiah 2:4)

26. Woe is _____! (Isaiah 6:5)

27. See eye to _____ (Isaiah 52:8)

28. Holier than _____ (Isaiah 65:5)

29. Weighed in the _____ (Daniel 5:27)

30. Salt of the _____ (Matthew 5:13)

31. Good for _____ (Matthew 5:13)

32. An eye for an _____, and a tooth for a _____ (Matthew 5:38)

33. Pearls before _____ (Matthew 7:6)

34. House _____ against itself (Matthew 12:25)

35. Fell by the _____ (Matthew 13:4)

36. Signs of the _____ (Matthew 16:3)

37. A den of _____ (Matthew 21:13)

38. Blood _____ (Matthew 27:6)

39. In his right _____ (Mark 5:15)

40. Physician, _____ thyself (Luke 4:23)

41. A law unto _____ (Romans 2:14)

42. The powers that _____ (Romans 13:1)

43. It is high _____ (Romans 13:11)

44. In the twinkling of an _____ (I Corinthians 15:52)

45. A _____ in the flesh (II Corinthians 12:7)

46. Labor of _____ (I Thessalonians 1:3)

47. The root of all _____ (I Timothy 6:10)

48. Keep the _____ (II Timothy 4:7)

49. Cover a _____ of sins (I Peter 4:8)

50. Bottomless _____ (Revelation 9:1, 20:1)

Answers

1. light 2. keeper 3. birthright, pottage 4. fat 5. milk, honey 6. bread 7. apple 8. breadth 9. heart 10. fool

11. voice 12. wailing 13. ghost 14. living 15. babes 16. desire 17. end 18. vain 19. depths 20. fall

21. vanities 22. sun 23. merry 24. snow 25. swords, plowshares 26. me 27. eye 28. thou 29. balances 30. earth

31. nothing 32. eye, tooth 33. swine 34. divided 35. wayside 36. times 37. thieves 38. money 39. mind 40. heal

41. themselves 42. be 43. time 44. eye 45. thorn 46. love 47. evil 48. faith 49. multitude 50. pit

Mythology

Test Your Mythology IQ

Legend has it that Alexander the Great always carried a treasured edition of Homer and that he put it under his pillow at night, along with his sword. When Alexander defeated the Persian king Darius, a golden casket studded with gems was among the booty. Inside that chest Alexander placed his edition of Homer, proclaiming, "There is but one thing in life worthy of so precious a casket." Classical mythology is indeed a treasure trove of literature, philosophy, and religion.

Knock, knock.

Who's there?

Electrolux.

Electrolux who?

Electrolux her father, but not her mother.

You would have to possess a high mythological IQ to understand the humor of that little knock-knock joke, which is based on a reader's knowledge of Aeschylus's *Oresteia*. When Agamemnon, king of Greece, returned from the Trojan War, his wife Clytemnestra murdered him in his bath. Their daughter, Electra, who remained loyal to her father, sought a fatal revenge against her mother.

To see how powerful your mythological literacy is, I've prepared a test of Olympian proportions. The world of classical mythology is essentially a human world. Realizing how splendid men and women could be, the Greeks and Romans made their gods and goddesses in their own images. Match the items in columns two and three with each god and goddess in column one:

Greek name	Latin name	Realm
1. Zeus	Ceres	agriculture
2. Poseidon	Cupid	fire and the forge
3. Hades/Pluto	Diana	hearth and home
4. Hera	Dis	king of gods and men
5. Phoebus Apollo	Faunus	love
6. Pallas Athena	Juno	love and beauty
7. Ares	Jupiter/Jove	messenger of gods
8. Aphrodite	Liber	moon and the hunt
9. Hermes	Mars	nature
10. Hephaestus	Mercury	queen of gods
11. Artemis	Minerva	sea
12. Demeter	Neptune	sun
13. Hestia	Phoebus Apollo	underworld

Greek name	Latin name	Realm
14. Bacchus/ Dionysus	Venus	war
15. Eros	Vesta	wine and revelry
16. Pan	Vulcan	wisdom

Now you are invited to hit a Homer. The following characters were all involved in the events of the Trojan War, chronicled in Homer's *Iliad* and other ancient works. Match each name in the first column with the appropriate description in the second:

17. Achilles   king of Troy

18. Agamemnon   queen of Troy

19. Andromache   leader of Greek forces

20. Astyanax   chief warrior for the Greeks

21. Ajax   second greatest Greek warrior

22. Cassandra   mother of Achilles

23.	Diomedes	best friend of Achilles
24.	Hector	greatest Trojan warrior
25.	Hecuba	wife of Hector
26.	Helen	son of Hector
27.	Iphigenia	"the face that launched a thousand ships"
28.	Laocoön	daughter of Agamemnon
29.	Menelaus	husband of Helen
30.	Nestor	judge of beauty contest
31.	Odysseus	Amazon killed by Achilles
32.	Paris	first man to land at Troy
33.	Patroclus	oldest and wisest of the Greeks
34.	Penthesileia	feigned madness to avoid the war
35.	Priam	went mad
36.	Protesilaus	loud-voiced herald
37.	Stentor	warned Trojans of Trojan horse
38.	Thetis	prophetess to whom no one listened

The following characters are all involved in Homer's *Odyssey*. Match each name in the first column with the appropriate description in the second:

39.	Aelus	hero of the *Odyssey*
40.	Antinous	wife of Odysseus
41.	Argus	son of Odysseus
42.	Calypso	beautiful, dangerous witch
43.	Circe	nymph who loved Odysseus
44.	Odysseus	Odysseus's dog
45.	Penelope	Theban prophet
46.	Polyphemus	fatal singers
47.	Scylla	arrogant suitor
48.	Sirens	king of the winds
49.	Telemachus	had 20/ vision
50.	Tiresias	sea monster

Answers

1. Jupiter/Jove, king of gods and men 2. Neptune, sea 3. Dis, underworld 4. Juno, queen of gods 5. Phoebus Apollo, sun 6. Minerva, wisdom 7. Mars, war 8. Venus, love and beauty 9. Mercury, messenger of gods 10. Vulcan, fire and the forge

11. Diana, moon and the hunt 12. Ceres, agriculture 13. Vesta, hearth and home 14. Liber, wine and revelry 15. Cupid, love 16. Faunus, nature 17. chief warrior for the Greeks 18. leader of Greek forces 19. wife of Hector 20. son of Hector

21. went mad 22. prophetess to whom no one listened 23. second greatest Greek warrior 24. greatest Trojan warrior 25. queen of Troy 26. "the face that launched a thousand ships" 27. daughter of Agamemnon 28. warned Trojans of Trojan horse 29. husband of Helen 30. oldest and wisest of the Greeks

31. feigned madness to avoid the war 32. judge of beauty contest 33. best friend of

Achilles 34. Amazon killed by Achilles 35. king of Troy 36. first man to land at Troy 37. loud-voiced herald 38. mother of Achilles 39. king of the winds 40. arrogant suitor

41. Odysseus's dog 42. nymph who loved Odysseus 43. beautiful, dangerous witch 44. hero of the *Odyssey* 45. wife of Odysseus 46. had 20/ vision 47. sea monster 48. fatal singers 49. son of Odysseus 50. Theban prophet

There's a God in Your Sentence

Of all the literary sources that feed into our English language, mythology is one of the richest. We who are alive today constantly speak and hear and write and read the names of the ancient gods and goddesses and heroes and heroines, even if we don't always know it.

Echo, for example, is an echo of a story that is more than two millennia old. Echo was a beautiful nymph who once upon a time aided Zeus in a love affair by keeping Hera, his wife, occupied in conversation. As a punishment for such verbal meddling, Hera confiscated Echo's power to initiate conversation and allowed her to repeat only the last words of anything she heard.

This was a sorry enough fate, but later Echo fell madly in love with an exceedingly handsome Greek boy, Narcissus, who, because of Echo's peculiar handicap, would have nothing to do with her. So deeply did the nymph grieve for her unrequited love, that she wasted away to nothing until nothing was left but her voice, always repeating the last words she heard.

The fate that befell Narcissus explains why his name has been transformed into words like *narcissism* and *narcissistic*, pertaining to extreme self-love. One day Narcissus looked into a still forest lake and beheld his own face in the water, although he did not know it. He at once fell in love with the beautiful image just beneath the surface, and he, like Echo, pined away for a love that could never be consummated.

Using the following descriptions, identify the gods and goddesses, heroes and heroines, and fabulous creatures that inhabit the world of classical mythology and the words that echo them:

1. One of the vilest of mythology's villains was a king who served the body of his young son to the gods. They soon discovered the king's wicked ruse, restored the dead boy to life, and devised a punishment to fit the crime. They banished the king to Hades, where he is condemned to stand in a sparkling pool of water with boughs of luscious fruit overhead; when he stoops to drink, the water drains away through the bottom of the pool, and when he wishes to eat, the branches of fruit sway just out of his grasp. Ever since, when something presents itself temptingly to our view, we invoke this king's name.

2. An adjective that means "merry, inspiring mirth" comes from the name the ancient Romans gave to the king of their gods because it was a happy omen to be born under his influence.

3. The frenetic Greek nature god was said to cause sudden fear by darting out from behind bushes and frightening passersby. That fear now bears his name.

4. The goddess of love and beauty gives us

many words from both her Greek and Roman names.

5. A Greek herald in Homer's *Iliad* was a human public address system, for his voice could be heard all over camp. Today, the adjective form of his name means "loud-voiced, bellowing."

6. The most famous of all of Homer's creations spent ten years after the fall of Troy wandering through the ancient world encountering sorceresses and cyclopses (with 20/ vision). The wily hero's name lives on in the word we use to describe a long journey or voyage marked by bizarre turns of events.

7. The hero Odysseus was tempted by mermaids who perched on rocks in the sea and lured ancient mariners to their deaths. Their piercing call has given us our word for the rising and falling whistle emitted by ambulances, fire engines, and police cars.

8. Another great Greek hero needed all his power to complete twelve exceedingly laborious labors. We use a form of his name to describe a mighty effort or an extraordinarily difficult task.

9. A tribe of female warriors cut off their right breasts in order to handle their bows more efficiently. The name of their tribe originally meant "breastless;" it now means a strong woman.

10. Because of its fluidity and mobility, quicksilver is identified by a more common label that is the Roman name for Hermes, the winged messenger of the gods. That name has also bequeathed us an adjective meaning "swift, eloquent, volatile."

Answers

1. tantalize—Tantalus
2. jovial—Jove
3. panic—Pan
4. aphrodisiac, hermaphrodite —
   Aphrodite; venereal, venerate—Venus
5. stentorian—Stentor
6. odyssey—Odysseus
7. siren—the sirens
8. Herculean—Hercules
9. Amazon—Amazons
10. mercury, mercurial—Mercury

Mythic Headlines

Ezra Pound once defined literature as "news that stays news." The plots spun out by many classic works of literature are as contemporary as today's headlines, especially as they are screamed in the tabloids. Just think what the *National Enquirer* and *Star* would do with the violent stories told in classical times if they had actually happened. For example, what story is reflected in this headline?

King Kills His Father, Then Marries Woman Old Enough to Be His Mother—and She Is!

You might know that this banner statement describes the story of Oedipus Rex, who, as things turned out, married the girl just like the girl that married dear old dad. That is, he blindly got hitched to his own mother, Jocasta. Now identify ten more ancient tales from these lurid modern-day headlines:

1. Invincible Greek Mercenary Done in by Arrow in His Heel

2. Queen Murders King in His Bath

3. Wiley Husband Slaughters Party Guests Hitting on His Wife

4. Witch Literally Turns Men Into Male Chauvinist Pigs

5. Crazy Strongman Murders Own Kids;
Later Chops Off Monster's Heads

6. Fiery God Punished Each Day
By Eagle Eating His Liver

7. Maniac Cooks King's Children;
Serves Them Up for Dinner

8. Self-Absorbed Hottie Guy
Drowns in His Own Image

9. Musical Genius Decides to Go
To Hell to Save Main Squeeze

10. Warrior Women Make
Clean Breast of Things

Answers

1. In the *Iliad*, Paris shot an arrow in Achilles' heel. 2. In the *Orestia*, Clytemnestra murdered her husband, Agamemnon, in his bath. 3. In the *Odyssey*, Odysseus returned home to Ithaca to slaughter his wife's suitors. 4. In the *Odyssey*, the witch Circe turned men into male chauvinist pigs. 5. Heracles (Hercules to the Romans) was driven mad by Hera and killed his own children.

6. The gods punished Prometheus by sending an eagle to gnaw on his liver, which grew back each day. 7. Tantalus cooked up and served the children of the King. 8. Narcissus leapt into a pond and drowned in his own image. 9. Orpheus went down to Hades to rescue his love, Eurydice. 10. The Amazon women had their right breasts cut off in order to better shoot their arrows.

Shakespeare

Living Will

Name a play written by Bartley Campbell. Of course you can't, nor can just about anyone else alive today. Yet Campbell (1843–1888) was a popular American playwright whose giant ego towered above his talent. His professional stationery depicted two portraits on the letterhead—Bartley Campbell on one side and William Shakespeare on the other—linked by the words, "A friendly rivalry." Today Campbell, a legend in his own mind, is forgotten, while Shakespeare endures and prevails as the one big gun in the canon of English literature who has no rival.

William Shakespeare is the darling of readers, playgoers, and critics alike. The critical work directly about the Bard or in some way relevant to him could constitute a library, and in fact does: the superb 280,000-volume Folger Library in Washington, D. C. Even if you somehow devoured that collection, you would still have to read 3,000 new discussions of Shakespeare each year to keep up with the new scholarship.

As the Huntsman in *King Henry VI* says, "This way, my lord, for this way lies the game." Here's an untrivial quiz on a far-from-trivial author. Supply the basic facts about Shakespeare's life and works that the following twenty questions ask for:

1. List the dates of Shakespeare's birth and death.

2. In what town and country was Shakespeare born?

3. Name the monarchs who reigned in Shakespeare's country during his lifetime.

4. Name Shakespeare's wife. "Mrs. Shakespeare" is not acceptable.

5. How many children did the Shakespeares have?

6. With what theater was Shakespeare most intimately connected?

7. What was the name of Shakespeare's acting company?

8. What is the importance of the following lines (in the original spelling)?

Good frend for Jesus' sake forbeare,
To digg the dust enclosed heare!
Blest be ye man yt spares thes stones,
And curst be he yt moves my bones.

9. One of Shakespeare's contemporaries rightly foresaw the magnitude of the Bard's achievement when he wrote of Shakespeare: "He was not of an age, but for all time!" Name the writer of that sentence.

10. How many plays did Shakespeare write?

11. What are the three categories by which the plays are generally classified?

12. Into how many acts is each play traditionally divided?

13. In what verse form did Shakespeare write his plays?

14. What do we call the first edition of Shakespeare's collected works?

15. Some scholars believe that Shakespeare didn't write Shakespeare. Name three people who supposedly ghostwrote for the Bard.

16. How many sonnets are in Shakespeare's sonnet sequence?

17. How many lines are in a typical Shakespearean sonnet?

18. In what poetic meter are the sonnets written?

19. Identify the plays begun by each of the following lines:

a. Now is the winter of our discontent
   Made glorious summer by this son of
      York:

b. Two households, both alike in dignity,
   In fair Verona, where we lay our scene,
   From ancient grudge break to new
      mutiny,
   Where civil blood makes civil hands
      unclean.

c. Hence! home, you idle creatures, get you
      home!
   Is this a holiday?

d. If music be the food of love, play on

e. Who's there?

f. When shall we three meet again?
   In thunder, lightning, or in rain?

20. Name the Shakespearean heroes with whom each of the following enemies contended: a. Iago b. Macduff c. Laertes and Claudius d. Hotspur e. Octavius Caesar f. Richmond g. Brutus and Cassius.

As Belarius exclaims in *Cymbeline*, "The game is up!" It's now time to consult the answers.

Answers

1. and 2. Shakespeare was baptized in Holy Trinity Church in the English village of Stratford-upon-Avon on April 26, 1564, and was probably born three days earlier. He died in Stratford on April 23, 1616. 3. Elizabeth I and James I. 4. Anne Hathaway. 5. Three: Susanna and the twins Hamnet and Judith.

6. The Globe. 7. For most of his career, Shakespeare was a member of the Lord Chamberlain's Company, later known as the King's Men. 8. These words are the epitaph on Shakespeare's grave in the chancel of the Holy Trinity Church. 9. Ben Jonson. 10. Thirty-seven.

11. Tragedies, comedies, and histories. 12. Five. 13. Blank verse: unrhymed iambic pentameter. 14. The First Folio. 15. The everchanging slate of candidates include Sir Walter Raleigh; Edward Devere, the Earl of Oxford; Francis Bacon; Christopher Marlowe; Mary Spenser Herbert; and the Earl of Essex.

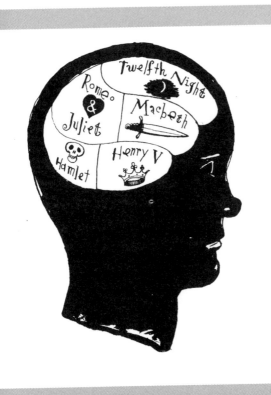

16. 154. 17. Fourteen. 18. Iambic pentameter, as in the plays. 19. a. *Richard III*; b. *Romeo and Juliet*; c. *Julius Caesar*; d. *Twelfth Night*; e. *Hamlet*; f. *Macbeth*. 20. a. Othello; b. Macbeth; c. Hamlet; d. Prince Hal (Henry V); e. Antony; f. Richard III; g. Julius Caesar.

Bomb-Bard-Ment

Now that you've taken a fairly straightforward quiz about William Shakespeare, prepare yourself for some trick questions. Because these posers are fraught with snares, delusions, and arcane knowledge, do not expect to get many of them right. Still, you'll find that the answers will make fascinating reading:

1. What do the following sentences have in common?

> *We all make his praise.*
> *I swear he's like a lamp.*
> *"Has Will a peer?" I ask me.*
> *Ah, I speak a swell rime.*
> *Wise male. Ah, I sparkle!*

2. How do Shakespeare's birth and death days relate to St. George and Miguel de Cervantes?

3. Who is the Merchant of Venice?

4. In the famous balcony scene from *Romeo and Juliet*, Juliet says, "O Romeo, Romeo! wherefore art thou Romeo?" What does *wherefore* mean?

5. How many times does the word *witch* appear in the dialogue of *Macbeth*?

6. When Cleopatra's lover asked her if she was in love with him, she answered, "Oh, Marc, I am!" Whether or not you caught the pun on "Omar Khayyam," correctly spell Marc's last name.

7. What character speaks the greatest number of lines in Shakespeare's plays?

8. What play contains the greatest number of Shakespearean lines? What play contains the smallest number?

9. What do these plays have in common? *Love's Labour's Lost, The Taming of the Shrew, A Midsummer Night's Dream,* and *Hamlet*

10. What do these plays have in common? *The Merchant of Venice, As You Like It, Twelfth Night,* and *Cymbeline*

11. "All the world's a stage . . . and one man in his _____ plays many parts." Provide the missing word. In what play does this famous speech appear? Explain how in the same play a male plays a female who plays a male who plays a female.

12. So you think you know your Shakespeare and can quote his lines with exquisite accuracy? Examine these five Shakespearean quotations and provide the missing words:

   a. "Alas, poor Yorick! I knew him _____" (*Hamlet*)

   b. "To _____ the lily" (*King John*)

   c. "All that _____ is not gold" (*The Merchant of Venice*)

   d. "_____ will have his day" (*Hamlet*)

   e. "To the _____ born" (*Hamlet*)

13. Are Shakespeare's sonnets addressed to a man or a woman?

14. What do the following words have in common?: *auspicious, bedroom, critic, dwindle, frugal, generous, majestic, obscene, submerge*

Answers

1. Each of the five sentences is an anagram of *William Shakespeare*, and each uses all the letters in his name. 2. Shakespeare was almost certainly born on April 23—St. George's Day—in 1564, and he died on the same day fifty-two years later, the same day on which the Spanish writer Miguel de Cervantes died. 3. Antonio, not Shylock. 4. "Why," not "where." (Think about the cliché "the whys and wherefores.") Thus, the spoken stress should be placed on *Romeo*, not *art*. 5. Only twice, I, 3, 6: "Aroint thee, witch!" and IV, 1, 23: "Witch's mummy." While the word *witch* appears many times in the stage directions, the lines of the play generally refer to the witches as "weird sisters."

6. Antony, not Anthony. 7. With a total of 1,422 lines, an actor playing Hamlet has more to learn than one playing any other single part in a single play by Shakespeare. But the character who speaks the greatest

number of lines in Shakespeare is Sir John Falstaff—1,178 in *Henry IV*, Parts I and II, and an additional 436 lines in *The Merry Wives of Windsor*, for a total of 1,614 lines. 8. *Hamlet*, with 3,931 lines, is the longest of Shakespeare's plays, and *The Comedy of Errors*, with 1,778, is the shortest. But the answer to the question of what play contains the smallest number of Shakespearean lines is not *The Comedy of Errors*. That's because Shakespeare collaborated with other playwrights on *Henry VIII* (to which he contributed 1,167 lines), *Pericles* (1,140 lines), and *The Two Noble Kinsmen*, which he wrote with John Fletcher and to which he contributed 1,131 lines. 9. Each play contains a play within a play. 10. Each play involves a woman who disguises herself as a man.

11. *Time*, not *life*. Most people say Hamlet,

but it is Jaques who delivers this speech in *As You Like It* (Act II, scene 7). In the earliest productions of Shakespeare's plays, only men and boys were allowed into the theater companies. In *As You Like It*, a male played the part of Rosalind, who, in the story, flees to the Forest of Arden disguised as a young man, who then pretends to be a man in order to help her paramour, Orlando, practice his wooing. 12. a. *Horatio*, not *well*; b. *paint*, not *gild*; c. *glisters*, not *glitters*; d. *dog*, not *every dog*; e. *manner*, not *manor*. 13. Both. Most were addressed to a young man, but approximately the last 20 percent were addressed to a woman. 14. They are among the more than 1,700 words invented by Shakespeare, who, "bethumpt with words," *(King John)* was truly "a man of fire-new words" *(Love's Labour's Lost)*.

A Man of Many Titles

William Shakespeare was a busy and prolific writer who, in twenty-five years, turned out thirty-seven long plays and co-authored several others, yet he still found time to provide titles for their books to generations of authors who return again and again to the well of his felicitous phrasing.

Take *Macbeth*, for example. Near the end of the play, Macbeth expresses his darkening vision of life: "It is a tale / Told by an idiot, full of sound and fury, / Signifying nothing." Centuries later, William Faulkner purloined a phrase from that speech for his novel *The Sound and the Fury*, which is indeed told by an idiot, Benjy Compson. Earlier in the play one of the witches chants, "By the pricking of my thumbs, / Something wicked this way comes." Agatha Christie plucked the first line and Ray Bradbury the second as titles of their bestsellers. Other steals from just the one play *Macbeth* include Robert Frost's "Out, Out—," Rose Macaulay's *Told by an Idiot*, Ellis Middleton's *Vaulting Ambition*, Adrienne Rich's *Of Woman Born*, Ngaio Marsh's *Light Thickens*, Anne Sexton's *All My Pretty Ones*, Alistair MacLean's *The Way to Dusty Death*, Edward G. Robinson's *All Our Yesterdays*, Philip Barry's *Tomorrow and Tomorrow*, Malcolm Evans's *Signifying Nothing*, and John Steinbeck's *The Moon is Down*.

Clearly, William Shakespeare was one of the most generous souls who ever set quill to parchment. Although he himself was never granted a title, he freely granted titles to others. Identify the literary titles plucked from the following lines:

1. How beauteous mankind is! O brave new
   world that has such people in't!
   —The Tempest, V, 1, I 183

2. The ears are senseless that should give us
      hearing,
   To tell him his commandment is fulfill'd,
   That Rosencrantz and Guildenstern are
      dead.
   Where should we have our thanks?
   —Hamlet, V, 2, 369

3. Now is the winter of our discontent
   Made glorious summer by the son of York;
   And all the clouds that low'rd upon our
      house
   In the deep bosom of the ocean buried.
   —Richard III, I, 1, 1

4. There are no tricks in plain and simple
      faith;
   But hollow men, like horses hot at hand,
   Make gallant show and promise of their
      mettle;
   —Julius Caesar, IV, 2, 22

5. Art thou any more than a steward? Dost thou think because thou art virtuous there will be no more cakes and ale?
    —Twelfth Night, II, 3, 114

6. When to the sessions of sweet silent thought
    I summon up remembrances of things past,
    I sigh the lack of many a thing I sought,
    And with old woes new wail my dear time's waste;
    —Sonnet XXX

7. And Caesar's spirit, ranging for revenge,
    With Ate by his side come hot from hell,
    Shall in these confines with a monarch's voice
    Cry 'Havoc,' and let slip the dogs of war,
    —Julius Caesar, III, 1, 270

8. The sun's a thief, and with his great attraction
    Robs the vast sea; the moon's an arrant thief,
    And her pale fire she snatches from the sun;
    —Timon of Athens, IV, 3, 436

9. What may this mean,
   That thou, dead corse, again in complete
      steel,
   Revisits thus the glimpses of the moon;
      —Hamlet, I, 4, 51

10. Men at some time are masters of their
      fates;
    The fault, dear Brutus, is not in our stars,
    But in ourselves, that we are underlings.
      —Julius Caesar, 1, 2, 139

Answers

1. *Brave New World*, Aldous Huxley 2. *Rosencrantz and Guildenstern are Dead*, Tom Stoppard 3. *The Winter of Our Discontent*, John Steinbeck 4. "The Hollow Men," T. S. Eliot 5. *Cakes and Ale*, W. Somerset Maugham

6. *Remembrance of Things Past*, Marcel Proust 7. *The Dogs of War*, Frederick Fotrsyth 8. *Pale Fire*, Vladimir Nabakov 9. *The Glimpses of the Moon*, Edith Wharton 10. *Dear Brutus*, James Barrie

Not a Passing Phrase

Oscar Wilde once quipped, "Now we sit through Shakespeare in order to recognize the quotations." Unrivaled in so many other ways in matters verbal, Shakespeare is unequaled as a phrasemaker. "All for one, one for all," and "not a creature was stirring—not even a mouse," wrote Alexandre Dumas in *The Three Musketeers* and Clement Clark Moore in *A Visit From St. Nicholas*. But Shakespeare said them first — "One for all, or all for one we gage" in *The Rape of Lucrece* and "not a mouse stirring" in *Hamlet*.

A student who attended a performance of *Hamlet* came away complaining that the play "was nothing more than a bunch of clichés." The reason for this common reaction is that so many of the memorable expressions in *Hamlet* have become proverbial. In that one play alone were born "brevity is the soul of wit"; "there's the rub"; "to thine own self be true"; "it smells to heaven"; "the very witching time of night"; "the primrose path"; "though this be madness, yet there is method in't"; "dog will have his day"; "the apparel oft proclaims the man"; "neither a borrower nor a lender be"; "frailty, thy name is woman"; "something is rotten in the state of Denmark"; "more honored in the breach than the observance"; "hoist with his own petard"; "the lady doth protest too much"; "to be, or not to be"; "sweets to the sweet"; "to the manner born"; "in my heart of hearts"; "yeoman's service"; and "more in sorrow than in anger."

Cudgel thy brains to complete these expressions that first saw the light in the other plays of William Shakespeare:

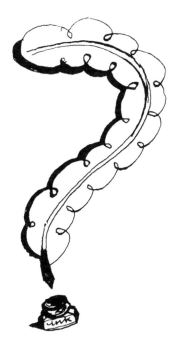

1. all the world's a _____ (*As You Like It*, II, 7, 139)

2. as good _____ would have it (*The Merry Wives of Windsor,* (III, 5, 72)

3. the better part of valor is _____ (*Henry IV,* Part 1, V, 4, 120)

4. a blinking _____ (*The Merchant of Venice,* II, 9, 54)

5. break the _____ (*The Taming of the Shrew,* I, 2, 262)

6. breathed his _____ (*Henry VI,* Part 3, V, 2, 40)

7. come full _____ (*King Lear,* V, 3, 174)

8. the course of true love never did run _____ (*A Midsummer Night's Dream,* I. 1. 134)

9. eaten me out of house and _____ (*Henry IV, Part 2,* II, 1, 67)

10. every _____ a king (*King Lear,* IV, 6, 107)

11. for _____ sake (*Henry VIII,* Prologue, 23)

12. a foregone _____ (*Othello,* III, 3, 428)

13. the green-eyed _____ (*Othello,* III, 3, 166)

14. have seen better _____ (*As You Like It*, II, 7, 120)

15. household _____ (*Henry V*, IV, 3, 52)

16. if music be the food of love, _____ (*Twelfth Night*, I, 1, 1)

17. infinite _____ (*Antony and Cleopatra*, II, 2, 236)

18. an itching _____ (*Julius Caesar*, IV, 3, 10 and12)

19. laid on with a _____ (*As You Like It*, I, 2, 94)

20. laugh yourselves into _____ (*Twelfth Night*, III, 2, 73)

21. loved not _____ but too well (*Othello*, V, 2, 344)

22. masters of their _____ (*Julius Caesar*, I, 2, 139)

23. melted into air, into thin _____ (*The Tempest*, IV, 1, 150)

24. milk of human _____ (*Macbeth*, I, 5, 17)

25. more sinned against than _____ (*King Lear*, III, 2, 60)

26. neither rhyme nor _____ (*The Comedy of Errors*, II, 2, 48)

27. not _____ an inch (*The Taming of the Shrew*, Ind. 1, 11)

28. one fell _____ (*Macbeth*, IV, 3, 219)

29. a pair of star-_____ lovers (*Romeo and Juliet*, Prologue, 6)

30. parting is such sweet _____ (*Romeo and Juliet*, II, 2, 184)

31. a plague on both your _____ (*Romeo and Juliet*, III, 1, 95)

32. pomp and _____ (*Othello*, III, 3, 354)

33. a pound of _____ (*The Merchant of Venice*, IV, 1, 307)

34. the quality of mercy is not ____ (*The Merchant of Venice*, IV, 1, 184)

35. salad _____ (*Antony and Cleopatra*, I, 5, 73)

36. short _____ (*Richard III*, III, 4, 97)

37. a sorry _____ (*Macbeth*, II, 2, 22)

38. [a] spotless _____ (*Richard II*, I, 1, 178)

39. strange _____ (*The Tempest*, II, 2, 40)

40. too much of a good _____ (*As You Like It*, IV, 1, 124)

41. a tower of _____ (*Richard III*, V, 3, 12)

42. uneasy lies the head that wears a ___ (*Henry IV,* Part 2, III, 1, 31)

43. the most unkindest _____ of all (*Julius Caesar*, III, 2, 183)

44. wear my heart upon my _____ (*Othello* I, 1, 64)

45. what ___ these mortals be (*A Midsummer's Night Dream*, III, 2, 115)

46. what the _____! (*The Merry Wives of Windsor*, III, 2, 15)

47. what's done is _____ (*Macbeth*, III, 2, 12)

48. wild-goose _____ (*Romeo and Juliet*, II, 4, 65)

49. with bated _____ (*The Merchant of Venice*, I, 3, 125)

50. the world's mine _____ (*The Merry Wives of Windsor*, II, 2, 3)

Answers

1. stage 2. luck 3. discretion 4. idiot 5. ice 6. last 7. circle 8. smooth 9. home 10. inch

11. goodness 12. conclusion 13. monster 14. days 15. words 16. play on 17. variety 18. palm 19. trowel 20. stitches

21. wisely 22. fates 23. air 24. kindness 25. sinning 26. reason 27. budge 28. swoop 29. crossed 30. sorrow

31. houses 32. circumstance 33. flesh 34. strained 35. days 36. shrift 37. sight 38. reputation 39. bedfellows 40. thing

41. strength 42. crown 43. cut 44. sleeve 45. fools 46. dickens 47. done 48. chase 49. breath 50. oyster

Classic Literary Lovers

This last game brings together the worlds of the Bible, Greek mythology, and William Shakespeare. As a kind of review of the literary span of this book, here's a quiz about the couples who couple in classic stories:

"The war between the sexes is the only one in which both sides regularly sleep with the enemy," observed Quentin Crisp. "Love is the triumph of imagination over intelligence," quipped H.L. Mencken. Whatever your opinion about love, literature swirls with it, and we often draw our images of love from the books we read, most deeply from the ancient books.

Starting with Adam and Eve, the Bible has chronicled many a married couple. Match the biblical husbands on the left with their biblical wives on the right. For extra credit, can you explain why there is one less husband than wife?

Abraham	Bathsheba
Ahasuerus	Dinah
Ananias	Esther
Aquila	Gomer
Boaz	Leah
Hosea	Mary
Isaac	Priscilla
Jacob	Rachel
Joakim	Rebecca
Joseph	Ruth
Moses	Sapphira
Shechem	Sarah
Uriah	Susanna
	Zipporah

Now let's enlist a list of classical couples.
Match each mythological man with each mythological woman:

Aeneas	Clytemnestra
Agamemnon	Dido
Deucalion	Deianeira
Hades	Echo
Hercules	Eurydice
Narcissus	Galatea
Oedipus	Jocasta
Orpheus	Persephone
Pygmalion	Pyrrha
Pyramus	Thisbe

Have you heard the one about the young couple in a Shakespeare play who went out to dinner? It ended up that Romee owed what Julie et. Now join together these husbands and wives and lovers who people the plays of William Shakespeare:

Antony   Audrey
Benedick   Beatrice
Brutus   Cleopatra
Ferdinand   Cressida
Florizel   Desdemona
Hamlet   Katharina
Henry V   Katharine
Oberon   Miranda
Duke Orsino   Ophelia
Othello   Perdita
Petruchio   Portia
Touchstone   Titania
Troilus   Viola

Answers

Bible:
Abraham/Sarah, Ahasuerus/Esther,
Ananias/Sapphira, Aquila/Priscilla,
Boaz/Ruth, Hosea/Gomer, Isaac/Rebecca,
Jacob/Leah, Rachel (Jacob had two wives,
Genesis 29), Joakim/Susanna,
Joseph/Mary, Moses/Zipporah,
Shechem/Dinah, Uriah/Bathsheba

Mythology: Aeneas/Dido,
Agamemnon/Clytemnestra,
Deucalion/Pyrrha, Hades/Persephone,
Hercules/Deianeira, Narcissus/Echo,
Oedipus/Jocasta, Orpheus/Eurydice,
Pygmalion/Galatea, Pyramus/Thisbe

Shakespeare: Antony/Cleopatra,
Benedick/Beatrice, Ferdinand/Miranda,
Florizel/Perdita, Hamlet/Ophelia, Henry
V/Katharine, Oberon/Titania, Duke
Orsino/Viola, Othello/Desdemona,
Petruchio/Katharina, Touchstone/Audrey,
Troilus/Cressida